# WITLEY COURT AND G

## ROGER WHITE

## INTRODUCTION

Once one of England's great country houses, Witley Court was largely gutted by fire in 1937 and was subsequently stripped and abandoned. Yet, as a ruin, it remains deeply evocative; as the historian Christopher Hussey wrote in 1945, 'classic order in dissolution, set among rampant vegetation and under the open sky, is the very substance of romance'. Today it offers the rare opportunity to see the bones of a mansion that has grown over the centuries, from the substantial Jacobean house, based on a medieval manor house, through the expansion under the first Baron Foley and his son in the 1720s and 1730s and the addition of two massive porticos by Regency architect John Nash. It finally reached its peak of grandeur in the 1850s with the extensive remodelling commissioned by the first Earl of Dudley from Samuel Daukes.

Lord Dudley's immense wealth, generated almost entirely by his industrial enterprises in the West Midlands, enabled his family to live an extraordinarily opulent life, here and in their many other properties. It also funded the creation of an ornate formal garden at Witley designed by William Andrews Nesfield, the leading garden designer of his day. An army of servants was involved in servicing the property and family, further swollen during the lavish house parties attended by the Prince of Wales (later Edward VII) and his circle. The separation of the house into 'upstairs' and 'downstairs' areas is typical of great Victorian houses, and the sophisticated services are one of the most fascinating aspects of Witley.

Such a way of life was already a thing of the past when, on the night of 7 September 1937, the Head Keeper spotted flames spurting from the roof above the servants' rooms in the south-east corner of the great house. Fanned by a strong wind, the fire rapidly spread downwards into the splendid reception rooms on the main floor; by the following day, much of the house was a smouldering shell. Although the west side was unaffected, the then owner Sir Herbert Smith decided not to rebuild but to put the estate up for sale. Witley was never lived in again.

The framework of the South Parterre has recently been recreated to give a hint of its former Victorian glory, and the Perseus and Andromeda fountain at its centre – one of the grandest in Europe – has been restored to working order. The formal gardens are complemented by the surrounding landscape of parkland, woodland and wilderness gardens. The ensemble is completed by the Georgian parish church of St Michael and All Angels (not English Heritage), which boasts one of the finest interiors of its period in the country.

MUSEUM OF WORCESTER PORCELAIN

*The Prince of Wales and the Earl and Countess of Dudley in front of the North Portico, December 1884, with servants in attendance. Notice the lion statues, later moved to the South Portico, and the carpet on the steps*

# TOUR OF WITLEY COURT

Take the path from the Visitor Centre and go through the gate. To get the best distant view of the house, turn right and walk to the end of the path.

Witley Court and Church sit on the far side of the lake known as Front Pool, which was originally formed in the eighteenth century by damming an existing stream. Visitors would once have reached the house by a causeway across the lake, and later by the carriage drive which you can see in front of the buildings.

Retrace your steps to the gate and follow the path which then bears right and drops to cross the dam at the end of the lake.

## THE WOODLAND AND WILDERNESS GARDENS

The ornamental woodland known as the Wilderness was originally developed at some point between 1772 and 1793, with walks laid out along the banks of Front Pool and the Shrawley Brook, which flows out of it. The planting was predominantly deciduous, with oaks, sweet chestnut and beech. In the early nineteenth century a new curving drive was created through the woodland and across the north front of the house, with lodges where it met the public road, probably designed by John Nash or G S Repton (these are shown on the 1828 Ordnance Survey, and were replaced in 1888 by the existing lodges in French Second Empire style, designed by Henry Rowe of Worcester). In the 1870s and 1880s rhododendron walks were introduced and the valley below the dam was extensively planted with American ornamental trees and plants, along with a profusion of spring-flowering bulbs

and shrubs. Below the dam a footbridge took the path across the Shrawley Brook, reinstated in timber and stone in 1999. This extensive area of woodland was separated from the house in the sales that followed the fire of 1937, with many of the fine mature trees being felled. Altogether, about half the Wilderness was cleared to form paddocks. Work is now under way to replace the sycamore woodland that has grown up since then with the original mixed woodland and ornamental planting, together with new footpaths, viewing points and sites for sculpture.

At the far end of the dam turn right up the slope and cross the drive to reach the Forecourt. Alternatively, turn left and follow the ornamental walks through the valley; you will eventually rejoin the path up to the house.

*Above: The Ionic capitals of the South Portico*

*Left: A view in the woodland walks showing the rustic bridge across the Shrawley Brook*

*Opposite: The magnificent view of Witley Court and Church across Front Pool*

NATIONAL MONUMENTS RECORD

*Above: The massive Ionic columns of the North Portico, with its paving in squares of pink sandstone and black and white marble, seen before the fire of 1937*

*Right: The Entrance Hall today, looking towards the staircase*

*Opposite: The Entrance Hall in 1920, furnished with Georgian hall settees and Victorian sculpture. The main staircase rises at the far end*

## FORECOURT

The appearance of the house that you see in front of you now is largely the result of an extensive remodelling in the mid-nineteenth century. However, the bones are still those of the Jacobean house built around 1610-20, which already had twin towers and wings extending to left and right on this side. The right-hand wing originally contained the Long Gallery on its upper floor, which was later altered to create a top-lit Picture Gallery. Impressive though it now is, until the early nineteenth century the composition must have looked even more imposing from this side, since it was further extended to left and right by a pair of large eighteenth-century service wings and arcaded screen walls. These were demolished by John Nash, the celebrated architect to the Prince Regent, who also added the portico of six massive Ionic columns to the centre. He may have given the brick house a coating of white

stucco, which was then replaced, in the 1850s, by much more expensive Bath stone to match the portico. You can see where the stone has come away in places to reveal the original brick construction. The Victorian transformation, designed by Samuel Daukes for the first Earl of Dudley, gave the house the Italianate look made fashionable ten years earlier by Osborne House on the Isle of Wight. Daukes's internal reconstruction of the left-hand wing, from four floors to three, meant that the existing windows were at the wrong level, so on the courtyard side they were blocked up but given false glazing to correspond to the wing opposite.

Up on the slope to the right is the very fine Georgian church (not English Heritage), which is described at the end of the tour (see page 17).

## ENTRANCE HALL

*Climb the portico steps and walk through the centre door into the Entrance Hall.*

The site of the present Entrance Hall has been the heart of the house at Witley since medieval times, when the great hall of the manor house was here (remains of the early fourteenth-century vaulted undercroft still exist beneath the modern concrete floor). This was succeeded by the hall of the Jacobean house, which in turn became the Entrance Hall in successive remodellings. Here visitors would be greeted by

*A blocked Jacobean window, revealed by the fire*

*Right: The view through the house from the North Portico, giving a glimpse of the Perseus and Andromeda fountain beyond*

the staff or, if they were sufficiently important, by the owners themselves. Nash was responsible for turning it into a double-height room, running between the Dining Room to the left and the main staircase, which rose beyond the blocked opening to the right; note its cast-iron frame. The hall received its final remodelling and redecoration in the 1850s. Victorian photographs show it furnished with eighteenth-century hall settees (probably from the earlier house), potted palms and plenty of nineteenth-century marble sculpture. The staircase was an 'imperial' one, with a central flight which divided at a half-landing and returned in two flights to reach the balcony that ran around the hall at first-floor level. This in turn gave access to bedrooms and also to the top-lit Picture Gallery, occupying almost the whole of the first floor of the west wing where the Long Gallery had been. The bedrooms along the south side were reserved for important guests, especially royalty, while other visitors stayed in the guest

rooms in the west wing. In comparison with many of the other interiors, the hall decoration was restrained, with simple panelling on the walls (executed in 'Carton Pierre' – see panel) and a deeply beamed ceiling.

Almost all the decoration was destroyed by the fire, but sections of the panelling survive to the right of the door opposite the entrance. To the left of the same door is a blocked mullion-and-transom window in sandstone, a relic of the Jacobean house and a reminder that until about 1730 the centre block of the house was only one room thick; hidden behind panelling for two hundred years, the fire brought it to light again. On the inside of the north portico wall can be seen the supports for the balcony.

## WEST TOWER

To the left of the portico wall a well-preserved early seventeenth-century doorcase leads into the West Tower. In the seventeenth and eighteenth centuries this and the corresponding east tower contained staircases, vestiges of which remain between the second and third floors. More of the Carton Pierre decoration can be seen here and also laths to support plaster on the walls. In the Victorian house the Entrance Hall level of the west tower contained a room from which servants kept an eye out for visitors approaching up the Forecourt. Both towers are now internally braced with concrete ring-frames.

## CARTON PIERRE DECORATION

This was an early attempt at mass-production of decorative mouldings for walls and ceilings. It was invented in the mid-19th century by a Parisian plasterer called Mizière, and was similar to papier mâché but of a more refined composition, so that highly detailed mouldings could be created. The ingredients included shredded paper, glue, water, flour and 'whiting' – made from ground chalk. Sometimes alum (sulphate of aluminium and potassium) was added. This mixture was then boiled up and pressed into wooden or metal moulds. The resultant mouldings were glued onto the prepared plaster surfaces.

Carton Pierre came to be used extensively and in the most fashionable circles. It featured in the Louvre and the Palais Royal in Paris and, once English manufacturers had taken up the process, it was employed in the decoration of Sandringham House for the future King Edward VII. Eventually Carton Pierre was superseded by fibrous plaster, which was stronger and could be made in larger sections.

*Surviving Carton Pierre decoration in the West Tower*

## RED SITTING ROOM

*Cross the Entrance Hall and go through the arched doorway opposite. Continue through the small room which once contained the servants' stairs to reach the Red Sitting Room.*

The Red Sitting Room is one of the sequence of rooms added across the south side of the Jacobean house in the 1730s. This and the larger Red Room to the right would have been used as private sitting rooms. Surrounding the nineteenth-century doorway in the right-hand wall is the outline of the outer side of a seventeenth-century window, while in the adjacent corner are finely laid stone quoins (or cornerstones) – both indications that this was once an outside wall.

## RED ROOM

*Look through the doorway to your right.*

The site of the Red Room was originally a short wing projecting from the south-west corner of the Jacobean house. By turning and craning your neck upwards towards the upper section of the wall above you, you can begin to appreciate the complex changes in the roof structure over nearly three centuries.

## EAST TOWER

*Return to the Entrance Hall, turn right and walk to the far end. Go through the door in the portico wall into the East Tower.*

In the Jacobean house, this was another staircase tower. In the early nineteenth century the stairs were removed and the space at this level was remodelled as a circular vestibule, making it possible to enter the library in the east wing (predecessor to the Ballroom) without going through the Dining Room – the blocked door can be seen to your right. On Victorian plans this room is labelled 'Library'. In the 1937 fire, the tower acted as a kind of flue, up which the flames roared.

*Housemaids in their day dresses, probably during the owners' absence as the furniture in the background is dust-sheeted*

*The intimate Red Sitting Room in 1920. The alcoves can still be seen today*

*The Dining Room in 1920, as remodelled in the 1850s for entertaining small groups of guests and friends*

*A detail of an 1886 illustration of a country-house ball such as would have been held at Witley*

MARY EVANS PICTURE LIBRARY

NATIONAL MONUMENTS RECORD

## DINING ROOM

☞ *Return to the hall and turn left.*

Until the fire, a wall with tall double doors divided the hall from the Dining Room. Here the owners would dine on their own or with relatively small gatherings of guests and friends; for larger, more formal dinners the Ballroom would be used. Beneath the Dining Room was a spacious butler's pantry, from which the room was serviced at meal times via a small adjoining servery and staircase, the food being brought at the lower level from the main kitchen on the opposite side of the house.

In plan the Dining Room was an elongated octagon, originally formed at the beginning of the nineteenth century by John Nash, who seems to have decorated it in 'Etruscan' style. Soon after the first Earl of Dudley came into his inheritance in 1848 it was remodelled in Louis XV style, with the walls divided into round-arched panels in which doors alternated with great sheets of mirror glass. The moulded decorations were of Carton Pierre, some of which survives on the walls. A photograph of 1920 shows a white marble chimneypiece,

Victorian dining table and chairs, and elegant side tables (possibly Regency) on which were placed ornate candelabra. The windows overlook the East Parterre garden with the Flora fountain at its centre.

## BALLROOM

☞ *Walk through the archway in the north wall of the Dining Room.*

The Ballroom, again in Louis XV style, was undoubtedly the most magnificent room in the house, 21 metres (69 feet) long and extending almost the full length of the north-east wing. The ceiling, too, was higher than those of the other reception rooms, making it possible to light the room with eight enormous crystal chandeliers. The Ballroom replaced an equally splendid library and was created to accommodate glittering balls, dinners and other large-scale social gatherings. On these occasions the innumerable flickering candles would have been reflected in the vast plate-glass mirrors that lined the room, and would have caught the gold leaf on the sumptuous plaster ornament of walls and ceiling. At Christmas it is said that Lord Dudley had the Ballroom tree hung with precious jewellery, from which lady guests chose before they left the house.

The 1937 fire was particularly intense here, revealing the rivetted steel girders that supported the floor above and charring the window timbers.

## GREEN SALON

☞ *Continue through the Ballroom to the far end.*

At the opposite end of the Ballroom to the Dining Room, the Green Salon was another octagonal room, perhaps used by those taking a break from the dancing next door. Beyond it again was a small ante-room, which contained a staircase descending to a sunken bath in the basement, probably a relic of the Foley era.

*Right: The Ballroom with its gilded plasterwork and crystal chandeliers. The Green Salon can be glimpsed through the open doors at the far end.*

*A surviving Victorian fire grate at first-floor level*

*Right: The south front, inside the portico*

## DRAWING ROOM

☞ *Return to the Entrance Hall and go through the gap in the wall ahead.*

You are now back in the range of rooms added to the Jacobean house in the 1730s; to your left is a massive chimneystack that until then was on the outer wall. In the nineteenth century the Drawing Room was created out of two smaller eighteenth-century rooms, replacing the intervening wall with a pair of Ionic columns. The resulting room, with its gilded Louis XV-style panelling, was spacious but low-ceilinged. All the decoration was destroyed in the fire, but you can see the remains of two Victorian fire grates at first-floor level.

## LOOKING AT WITLEY COURT AS A RUIN

Great country houses have always been vulnerable to fire, and many splendid piles are now known to us only through paintings and engravings as a result. In previous centuries, fires often resulted in a rebuilding in the latest architectural taste, but after the First World War the confidence to do so was usually lacking, and a serious fire was more likely to result in immediate demolition. Even historic houses owned by the National Trust, Coleshill in Berkshire and Dunsland in Devon, were demolished after fires as recently as 1952 and 1967 respectively. The decision to restore Uppark in Sussex after the terrible fire of 1989 demonstrates how attitudes have changed, and how such houses are once again valued as vital pieces of the national heritage.

Ruins, however, can have their own special appeal, and the appreciation of them has been an important part of western culture since at least the sixteenth century, when visitors to Rome and its environs began to pay particular attention to the remains of classical antiquity. As a guidebook of the time observed, 'from the ruins we learn the greatness that was Rome'. In eighteenth-century England the ruins of great medieval monasteries such as Rievaulx exerted a growing fascination on poets, writers and men of taste generally. Ruins can set the romantic imagination free, prompting reflections on vanished glories; more prosaically they can, as at Witley Court, make it possible to analyse the structure of buildings that have grown and evolved over centuries in a way that would not be possible if they were still in perfect shape. Certainly the historian Christopher Hussey, writing in *Country Life* in 1945, just eight years after the great fire, seemed to like Witley better as a ruin:

*'The buildings and gardens of Witley Court are more pictorially romantic now than ever in their well-kept prime. Roofless and windowless, the sleek Victorian palace has been shocked into the kind of nightmare vitality that Piranesi gave his architectural dramas. Here in peaceful Worcestershire is a classic ruin to be enjoyed dry-eyed for its beauty alone, in which we can recapture something of the pleasing awe with which our forefathers discovered vestiges of the ancient world.'*

The Ruined Temple of Saturn in the Roman Forum, *painted by T Caffi, showing early 19th-century tourists*

*The Drawing Room, formed in the 1850s out of two smaller Georgian rooms. The columns in the centre mark the position of the outside wall of the Jacobean house*

*Recarved decoration above the Saloon door*

*Georgina, widow of the first Earl of Dudley, with her grandchildren (including the twin boys, born 1907) in the South Portico*

## SALOON

☞ *Go through the door at the far end of the Drawing Room.*

The bow-fronted Saloon is at the centre of the south, or garden, front of the mansion. In the eighteenth century it would have been an important room for socialising, although the addition of the massive portico outside must have made it rather dark. In Victorian times it came to be used mainly as a passage room leading to the garden. Some of the Carton Pierre decoration from that period survives.

## SOUTH PORTICO

☞ *Walk out of the Saloon into the Portico.*

Like the portico on the north front through which you entered the house, the South Portico was added by John Nash in the early nineteenth century. Eight columns wide and two deep, it has been described as 'probably the biggest of any country house in Britain'. The floor was originally paved in a design, thought to be of the signs of the zodiac, in pink sandstone and black and white marble, of which there are remains between some of the pillars. Above the door from the Saloon, the elaborate decoration was recarved in 1993 as a result of a private donation from Miss Barbara Mapstone of Cheltenham. The great columns of the Portico frame a fine view over the formal gardens.

*A view across the South Portico to the Michelangelo Pavilion and Conservatory. Note the windows at ground level, lighting the service quarters*

*The restored stable-yard clock-tower, built by Nash*

*The curving screen wall seen from the churchyard, above the service courts*

## SERVICE COURTYARD

☞ *Descend the steps and turn right.*

In the mid-nineteenth century a long curving wing was added by Samuel Daukes to connect the south-west corner of the house to the enormous new conservatory. Although only the outer wall now remains, it contained the servants' hall and other service rooms at the lower level, with the nursery, schoolroom and governess's accommodation above. The service courtyard is not yet open to the public, but it is possible to look into it through the lower windows at this point.

The service courtyard, which was known as the Kitchen Court or Back Court, was the usual access to the house for servants and tradesmen and also, on a day-to-day basis, members of the Dudley family. It was flanked by arcaded loggias which screened such subsidiary rooms as the gun room and game larder on the south and the laundry, drying rooms and kitchen maids' rooms on the north. A long passage led from the laundry out to the drying grounds, probably to ensure that the laundry maids were shielded from the attentions of the stable lads, for between the two lay the stable court (latterly including garage space for seven cars, workshops and an engine room) and an outer court with harness rooms and coach houses. The kitchen, which had previously been in the basement of the east wing, was moved to this position some time in the eighteenth century, when a long narrow range containing servants' rooms was also built. This was incorporated in the complex of three service courts created in the early nineteenth century by John Nash, which included the stable court with its attractive clock tower, recently restored. The whole service area was unaffected by the 1937 fire but was stripped out and allowed to fall into ruin in the 1940s.

## MICHELANGELO PAVILION

At the end of the wing, entrance to the Conservatory was provided by the elegant Michelangelo Pavilion, so-called because its design is loosely based on that of the Capitoline Museum in Rome, designed by the sculptor and painter Michelangelo Buonarotti in about 1539. Inside are a fine tessellated floor and niches for statues.

## CONSERVATORY

▸ *Walk round the corner and climb the steps into the Conservatory.*

The Conservatory, sometimes known as the Orangery, was one of the largest to be found in any English country house: thirteen bays long by five deep. It replaced a smaller detached conservatory in this position designed by Nash. Sheets of plate glass were fitted directly into the stonework of the arches without conventional window frames (fragments of glass can still be seen), while the whole enormous interior space was spanned by a great curved glass roof. Inside was a marble floor, some of which remains, and raised beds with stone edgings. The stone

baskets of flowers on the rear wall were carved by James Forsyth (who also carried out much of the other carving around the house), while the stone block near the centre once supported an ornamental urn. Exotic plants such as palm trees were kept alive with help from the conservatory's self-contained heating system, fuelled by the Dudleys' own coal. Although the building escaped the fire, reusable materials such as the lead and plate glass were subsequently stripped out and sold, leaving a roofless shell. Of the planting, only the large camellia on the rear wall remains from before 1937.

## LOUIS XVI COURT

▸ *Leave the Conservatory by the door at the far end and descend the steps into the Louis XVI Court.*

Fruit trees were trained up the walls of this sheltered area. The niche in the far wall contained a statue now at Harlaxton Manor, Lincolnshire. Behind the screen wall was the vast coal store, kept stocked at a level of 1,500 tons, since at peak times the mansion's elaborate heating system consumed as much as 30 tons a day. The coal was transported by water from the Black Country to Stourport-on-Severn, and then by cart to Witley, where two or three coalmen were employed to sort it by grade for fireplaces and furnaces.

*The Victorian conservatory in about 1870*

*The twin sons of the second Earl of Dudley, photographed in the conservatory with their sister Lady Alexandra (named after her godmother Queen Alexandra)*

*Left: The iron staircase leading from the Conservatory into the Louis XVI Court*

## THE FORMAL GARDENS

☞ *If you have ended the tour of the house at the Louis XVI Court, return to the South Portico.*

The dip below the south portico, where the Perseus and Andromeda fountain now is, may have been the site of the little village of Great Witley, since houses are shown here in a painting of about 1700 (see page 18). When the first Lord Foley (Thomas III) enlarged the mansion in the 1720s, giving it a new south front, he presumably decided that the village was too close and relocated it – a not unusual procedure at the time – since the houses are no longer there on Price's estate map of 1732. The area was then landscaped informally as part of a deer park, which is shown on a map of 1772. A later Lord Foley (Thomas VII) employed John Nash and Humphry Repton to reintroduce an element of formality, with

terracing and balustrading in the immediate vicinity of the house together with flowerbeds and simple parterres. When, in the 1850s, the Earl of Dudley had the house remodelled in Italianate style, he called in the leading garden designer W A Nesfield to provide an appropriately grand setting. This was implemented between 1854 and 1860.

## PERSEUS AND ANDROMEDA FOUNTAIN AND SOUTH PARTERRE

In front of Nash's South Portico Nesfield introduced a vast flight of steps, curving out to each side. At the foot is a pair of stone plinths which were originally surmounted by lions. From here a broad central path leads down to the large oval pool containing the spectacular Perseus and Andromeda fountain. The theme of

*The South Parterre, designed by W A Nesfield, as it was its Victorian heyday*

*One of the replica cupids*

*Left: The restored Perseus and Andromeda fountain*

the central sculptural group, which was carved in Portland stone by James Forsyth (1827–1910), is the classical myth of Perseus and Andromeda. Perseus, having obtained the head of Medusa with the help of his winged sandals and his helmet of invisibility, flies to the rescue of Andromeda; she has been chained to a

rock by the sea god Poseidon, angry at the suggestion that she is more beautiful than the sea nymphs. A sea monster threatens to devour her, but Perseus gets there first and carries her off on the back of the winged horse Pegasus. Rising out of the water to left and right are two cupids riding dolphins, replicas based on photographs of the lost originals.

The engineers for the fountain were Easton & Co, who had worked on other Nesfield commissions at Holkham Hall (Norfolk) and Castle Howard (Yorkshire). To supply the necessary water, 4,000 gallons (18,000 litres) were pumped from a nearby pool to a reservoir over half a mile away and 100 feet (30 metres) above the level of the house. The main jet, which shot from the sea monster's open mouth, is said to have reached a height of 120 feet (36 metres), and there were numerous

*Left: Andromeda*

*Georgina, Countess of Dudley, and friends in front of the Perseus and Andromeda fountain in the 1880s*

*The Golden Gates, now in Arizona, which once terminated the South Parterre*

*One of the pair of domed pavilions in the South Parterre*

*Right: The East Parterre and Flora fountain catching the last rays of the sun, as seen from the South Portico*

*Gardeners working in the East Parterre in 1910*

subsidiary jets and sprays, as can be seen in early photographs. In its Victorian heyday the fountain played twice a week.

As first laid out, the fountain was surrounded by a pattern of formal borders, outlined by stone kerbs, and evergreens (Portuguese laurels, cypresses and yew) clipped into pyramids and cones, which have been reinstated by English Heritage. The lie of the land meant that the pattern could be appreciated from either the portico or the windows of the house. Beyond the pool a cross-terrace is terminated at each end by an elaborate stone pavilion with classical columns but a vaguely Hindu-style roof, designed by Nesfield, probably with input from Samuel Daukes. The continuation of the parterre to the south, where the ground slopes upwards again, is enclosed by a low semicircular balustrade and ha-ha, which separates the garden from what was the park (now farm land). At the centre, on axis with the portico and fountain, was a set of magnificent gates in gilded wrought iron, exhibited at the Paris Exhibition in 1862 and erected here to commemorate Queen Victoria's Silver Jubilee in the same year; these are now in Arizona. From the site of the gates there is a fine panorama of the house and church.

*Walk back down towards the fountain and up the slope to the right of the house.*

## EAST PARTERRE

To the east of the house was a smaller garden containing a highly elaborate French-style parterre, which could be admired from the windows of the Ballroom. It featured flowing designs laid out with box and filled with coloured gravels and flowers. This garden also contained clipped evergreens, flowering shrubs and ornamental bowls filled with flowers. To the right was a long guilloche, or ribbon of flowers.

The focal point when viewed from the house was a fountain of Flora, goddess of Spring and of flowers, whose statue crowned the composition. Her figure holds a cornucopia or horn, intended to jet water, and around her are four Tritons (fish-tailed humans) blowing jets of water from conch shells. Smaller jets line the

circumference of the basin. The original Flora statue was broken some years ago when an attempt was made to remove it, and the fountain as a whole has been badly vandalised. In Witley's heyday under the Earls of Dudley, whenever there was a ball in progress, the windows would be thrown open and the gardens would be illuminated with hundreds of coloured lanterns.

EH COURTESY OF GREAT WITLEY & HILLHAMPTON PARISH COUNCIL

## THE CHURCH

*The parish church of St Michael and All Angels, although physically attached to the mansion, is the responsibility of the Parochial Church Council rather than English Heritage; it is maintained by the local community and the entrance charge to Witley Court does not contribute to its upkeep. It can be reached by the path from the forecourt.*

Witley Church has one of the finest eighteenth-century ecclesiastical interiors in the country and would be worth a long detour even if Witley Court did not exist. Although at first sight it looks like the private chapel of the house, it has always been the parish church, replacing a ruinous thirteenth-century building that had stood a little further west. The first Lord Foley planned a new church which was constructed after his death in 1733, at the expense of his widow, and consecrated in 1735. This had a brick exterior to match the house as it then was, and a plain interior; the architect may have been James Gibbs. Twelve years later the church was transformed within and without when the second Lord Foley bought some of the fittings from the recently demolished chapel of the Duke of Chandos's mansion at Canons, Edgware. This too, one of the most magnificent baroque interiors of its day, had originally been designed by Gibbs, who was brought in again to fit out the Witley interior, incorporating ceiling panels painted by Antonio Bellucci and windows painted by Joshua Price after designs by Francesco Sleter. Gibbs provided a design for an elaborate new vaulted ceiling, carried out not in the usual plaster but in papier mâché (then a recent invention) by Thomas Bromwich of Ludgate Hill, London, who probably added some of the rococo embellishments. Bellucci's paintings include the big central oval of the Ascension and smaller panels of cherubs with symbols of Christ's Passion, while Price's windows depict scenes from the life of Christ.

The 'transepts' to either side of the altar contain Foley family monuments. To the left is a handsome pedimented tablet to Thomas Foley I (died 1677), saved from the medieval church, while to the right is the vast pyramidal composition commemorating the first Lord Foley and his family. This was designed and carved in 1753 by Michael Rysbrack (1694–1770), perhaps the leading sculptor of his generation in England, whose incised signature can be found on the monument. It cost £2,000, a very large sum at that time. Most of the other fittings of the church – pews, pulpit, font – were introduced by Samuel Daukes for the first Earl of Dudley around 1861, replacing existing Georgian fittings which were then exiled to Fawley church near Henley-on-Thames. Daukes was also responsible for encasing the brick exterior in stone, so that it matched the newly encased mansion. In 1913 mosaics by Salviati & Co were incorporated into the reredos behind the altar.

The church was happily untouched by the fire but with the decline of the house into ruin it too became sadly neglected. Restoration began in 1965 on the initiative of the parishioners and in 1993–4 the whole of the interior, including Bellucci's panels, was cleaned. More work remains to be done as the parish's finances allow.

*The church incorporates ceiling panels by Antonio Belluci and painted glass by Joshua Price, all brought from the ducal chapel at Canons, Edgware*

*The monument to the first Baron Foley and his family, by J M Rysbrack*

EH COURTESY OF GREAT WITLEY & HILLHAMPTON PARISH COUNCIL

*The Dudley crest*

## EARLY HISTORY

Domesday Book of 1086 records the manor of Witley as belonging to Urso d'Abetot. By the mid-thirteenth century ownership had passed to the Cooksey family, and the remains of the vaulted chamber which still survive under the hall of the present house probably date from this period or a little later; it may have been the undercroft of a solar, or withdrawing room, at one end of the Great Hall of the medieval manor house. On the death of Thomas Cooksey in 1498 Witley descended to his cousin Robert Russell of Strensham. At this stage the manor comprised 300–400 acres (120–160 hectares), the manor house itself and the adjoining church. Little is known of the substantial new house Russell is said to have built soon after inheriting, although a deer park to the south is thought to have been enclosed in the first half of the sixteenth century.

In about 1610–20 the medieval house was rebuilt on a grander scale by a descendant of Robert Russell. Its appearance is recorded by a solitary late seventeenth-century painting of the south front, which shows the central door framed by a pair of massive chimneystacks and short projecting wings. The main range was crowned by a cupola, and behind rose the twin staircase towers that have remained such a prominent feature of Witley Court ever since. The painting shows large mullion-and-transom windows, with the exception of those on the ends of the wings which were of the so-called 'Ipswich' type. In the foreground were walled enclosures, one of them apparently used as a bowling green. To the left was the medieval church, with a cluster of village houses below. The house, which was built of brick with stone dressings, was designed on an H-plan, with long wings projecting on the north, or entrance, front. Of these, the west wing contained a Long Gallery on the first floor, while the east wing was given over to service accommodation.

During the Civil War, Witley was the residence of Sir William Russell, a Royalist

*Wimbledon House, Surrey (demolished 1720), an Elizabethan mansion which gives an idea of how the original entrance front at Witley may have looked*

*This late 17th-century painting is the only known view of the Jacobean Witley Court and depicts the south front. The medieval church is shown to the left, and the houses below may be the remains of Witley village cleared away in the 18th century*

supporter, High Sheriff of the county and Governor of Worcester. In 1652 he is recorded as being threatened with the forfeiture of the estate to Edward Harrison, to whom he was in debt. But the debt must have been paid as, two years later, Sir William gave the property to his son Thomas as a wedding present. In 1655, however, Thomas Russell sold the estate, including the 'impressive residence', to Thomas Foley of Stourbridge.

## WITLEY UNDER THE FOLEYS, 1655–1837

Thomas Foley, born in 1616 or 1617, was the son of Richard Foley of Dudley, who had laid the foundations of his family's fortunes in the iron industry. Richard began by selling nails, but he later became involved in their manufacture as a forge master. Foreign competition was stiff, and Richard determined to improve the method (at that time mainly hand-work) by which the nails were made. He is said to have travelled to Uppsala in Sweden to observe a nail-making machine, which he copied on his return to England. On a further visit to Sweden, for purposes of what would now be called industrial espionage, he gained entry to the nail works by pretending to be half-witted. He went on to become a rich and respected member of Dudley society, being elected mayor at the age of 36 and building an almshouse for the poor. He married twice, fathering thirteen children, and in 1630 moved to Stourbridge, where he had established forges.

His son Thomas further developed the business, doing well out of the Civil War by supplying iron cannons and their ballistics. Appropriately, he married Anne Browne of Spelmonden in Kent, daughter of the greatest gun manufacturer in the country, and inherited a half-share of his father-in-law's business in 1652. This contributed to his reputed annual income of £5,000 – an enormous sum at the time – and meant that he could well afford to buy the Witley estate. He was highly regarded by contemporaries, enjoying a reputation for 'just and blameless dealing, that all men he ever had to do with... magnified his great integrity and honesty which was questioned by none'.

*Thomas Foley I, the first of eight Thomases to own the Witley estate, and his wife Anne Browne*

Like his father, Thomas engaged in local philanthropy, endowing Oldswinsford Hospital in Stourbridge, which is still a flourishing school today. He became High Sheriff of Worcestershire in 1655, served as a Member of Parliament, and died in 1677.

Foley was the first of no fewer than eight Thomases to own the Witley estate. His son (Thomas II), who likewise served as High Sheriff and an MP, is thought to have carried out substantial work on the house, since in 1695 it was referred to (by William Camden's *Britannia*) as 'fair new-built'; it is possible that the work included replacing the original roof with the overhanging hipped roof shown in the painting. By 1689 he had acquired the six manors that make up Great Witley, totalling about 2,600 acres (1,050 hectares). His son (Thomas III), again Sheriff and MP, succeeded in 1700 and was created Baron Foley of Kidderminster in 1711. He enlarged the house significantly, adding an extra floor to the centre block and doubling its depth by filling the space between the existing wings on the south front. Short two-storey wings were added to left and right, and the resulting composition was given central emphasis by a projecting elliptical bow on this side. New parapets were extended around the roof, and bay windows were added to

*Bird's-eye impression of how the Jacobean house appeared, as seen in the painting opposite*

*Witley Court as enlarged in the early 18th century. The bow front can still be seen behind the South Portico*

*The second Baron Foley in his robes*

*Right: The Keeper's Lodge, or Deer Park House, demolished in about 1950*

*G S Repton's early 19th-century drawing of the north front before Nash added the portico and subtracted the flanking service blocks*

terminate the ends of the north wings. The architect of all these alterations is not known. Lord Foley extended the grounds by acquiring additional land to the north, and planted an imposing avenue on the approach from the east. He had intended to rebuild the medieval church but died in 1732 before work could begin, so this project fell to his widow and his son Thomas IV, the second Lord Foley. The architect of the new church, which was consecrated in 1735, may have been James Gibbs (1682–1750), better known as the designer of St Martin-in-the-Fields in London, the Radcliffe Camera in Oxford and the Senate House in Cambridge; he was certainly responsible for installing the windows and ceiling paintings brought from the Duke of Chandos's chapel at Cannons in 1747.

Thomas IV continued the work of transformation by creating a new axial approach from the north, via a causeway across a lake –

the Front Pool – formed by damming a stream; his father had already purchased the land for this in 1718, but the feature is not shown on Charles Price's estate map of 1732. The impact of Witley Court on the visitor arriving from the north was enhanced still further by the addition of new service blocks, connected to the house by curving walls and framed in turn by arcaded screen walls. The result, as recorded in an early nineteenth-century drawing by George Repton, must have been extremely impressive. The exact date of these additions is not known, and nor is the identity of the architect; it could have been Gibbs, although another candidate might be the prominent Palladian architect Henry Flitcroft, who at some point before 1762 designed the Keeper's Lodge (also known as Deer Park House) for the second Lord Foley. This not only acted as an eyecatcher in the view from the south side of the house, but also served as a shooting lodge and a home for the head gamekeeper and his family. During the nineteenth century its

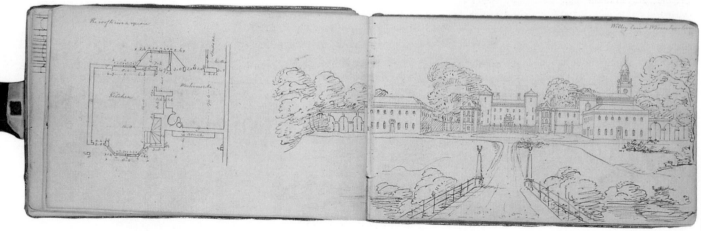

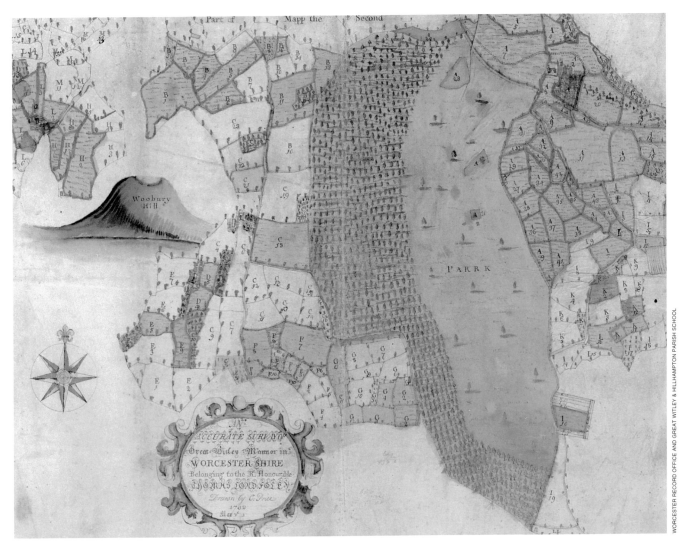

handsome portico became a useful grandstand from which sporting events could be viewed. By 1938 this attractive building had become derelict, and in about 1950 it was demolished.

When the second Lord Foley died a bachelor in 1766 the title became extinct and the estate passed to his second cousin, Thomas V, of Stoke Edith near Hereford. He, too, continued the family tradition of parliamentary service, and in 1776 was elevated to the peerage as Baron Foley 'of the second creation'. Sadly, his two elder sons embittered his later years with their dissipation. His heir, Thomas VI, was dubbed 'Lord Balloon' after an incident in which a hot-air balloon got out of control in the gardens of his London house. He achieved high office as a Privy Councillor and Lord Lieutenant of Worcestershire, but the contemporary Royal

Register noted that he had also, 'by a most rapid course of debauchery, extravagance and gambling, involved himself in a state of distress from the misery and disgrace of which he can never be extricated'. As a result of his behaviour he was disinherited by his father, and under him the family fortune was badly eroded.

Thomas VII, the third and only surviving son of Thomas VI, succeeded his profligate father in 1793, aged only thirteen, but in 1806 he was able to restore his financial position by marrying a daughter of the second Duke of Leinster, Ireland's premier peer. This may

*Charles Price's estate map of 1732. The house can be seen at the top right with the deer park lying to the west*

*Thomas VI, second Baron Foley, of the second creation, known as 'Lord Balloon'*

21

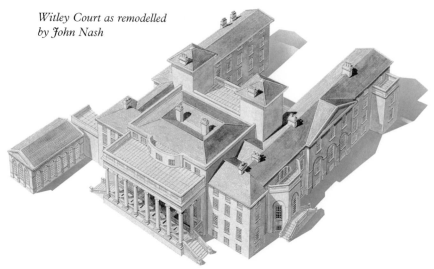

*Witley Court as remodelled by John Nash*

*Below: C R Cockerell's sketches and notes of Witley, showing the uses of the principal rooms in 1821*

*Wax medallion of John Nash*

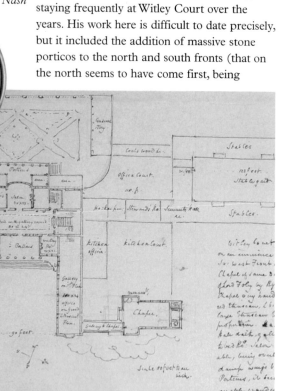

have enabled him to commission John Nash (1752–1835), the leading Regency architect, to design a succession of ambitious alterations. Nash was on friendly terms with the family, staying frequently at Witley Court over the years. His work here is difficult to date precisely, but it included the addition of massive stone porticos to the north and south fronts (that on the north seems to have come first, being

referred to in print in 1814); the raising of the wings so that the roof-line corresponded with the cornice on the porticos; and rebuilding the roof to a flatter pitch with overhanging 'Tuscan' eaves. It is possible that he was responsible for the application of a coat of white stucco to the whole exterior to mask the successive alterations of two centuries (Witley was referred to in 1814 as 'an immense white building'), since this was a material he used extensively elsewhere, except that a drawing of about 1800 appears to show the house already stuccoed.

The interior was replanned around the central gallery that Nash favoured in large houses, and the east wing was rebuilt. Here Nash created a sequence of rooms, including a dining room and library, which are known only through notes made by the great neoclassical architect C R Cockerell when he visited Witley in December 1821. Cockerell, who generally disapproved of Nash's work, described these interiors as 'red Etruscan, & bronze & marble in very coarse & vulgar taste, coved rooms with large Etruscan heroes, chariots & ill drawn, hot & disagreeable in color & proportion'. In reality Nash's interiors were probably good and characteristic examples of the sumptuous Regency taste which he had used elsewhere, above all for the Prince Regent. He also demolished the service blocks on the north front and replaced them with new accommodation around two courtyards at the south-west corner of the house. Finally, in 1828, George Repton (architect son of the celebrated landscape gardener Humphry Repton, and Nash's one-time assistant) built kennels to house Lord Foley's pack of hounds, designed as interlocking octagonal pavilions and exercise yards; these stood in the park well to the west of the mansion. Humphry Repton himself appears to have been consulted on the landscaping, although no documentation survives.

Despite his advantageous marriage, in 1810 Lord Foley was forced to raise a loan of £24,000 from Nash on the security of Foley House in London, although in 1812 the architect is said to have paid him the huge sum of £70,000 for the house, which stood in the way of the new street Nash was creating between Regent's Park and Carlton House in Pall Mall. Nevertheless, within four years of Foley's death in 1833, his son (Thomas VIII) was

*J Wood's view of Witley from the south-east in 1843, still as left by Nash and Repton*

*John William Ward, first Earl of Dudley*

*Queen Adelaide, widow of William IV, by Franz Winterhalter*

*A view of Dudley and its ironworks in 1853*

obliged to sell the Witley estate for £890,000 to the trustees of William Humble Ward, so bringing the long Foley connection to an end.

## WITLEY'S VICTORIAN HEYDAY

In 1837 the new owner of Witley, William Humble Ward (1818–85), eleventh Baron Ward of Birmingham, was still a minor. Even so, he was one of the richest individuals in England – and therefore, at that time, in the world. As with the Foleys, the wealth was based on West Midlands industry, but in this case from the technical innovations of the Industrial Revolution. He was heir to the income from over 200 mines in the Black Country, from which were extracted coal, iron, limestone and fireclay. He also owned iron-smelting works, chemical factories and a railway construction business, which together generated an annual income of some £100,000 (approximately £4.5 million in today's terms). Ward had inherited these vast assets in 1833 from a distant relation, John William Ward, first Earl of Dudley and a former Foreign Secretary. Known as 'the Lorenzo of the Black Country' (presumably in reference to Lorenzo de Medici), the earl died insane, conversing with himself in two voices, one falsetto and one bass.

Young Lord Ward did not come into his full inheritance until the age of 28, and meanwhile he lived at the family home of Himley Hall, near Stourbridge. After necessary repairs Witley Court was let, most notably (1843–46) to Queen Adelaide, widow of King William IV. She was a popular figure locally, paying for the building of the first village school and often to be seen out and about in her carriage. After her departure Lord Ward moved in. In 1851 he married a society beauty, Selina Constance de Burgh, but tragically she died in childbirth the same year. Soon afterwards, perhaps as a way of mitigating his grief, Ward began to plan a major transformation of Witley Court and its surroundings, which was duly carried out between 1854 and 1860.

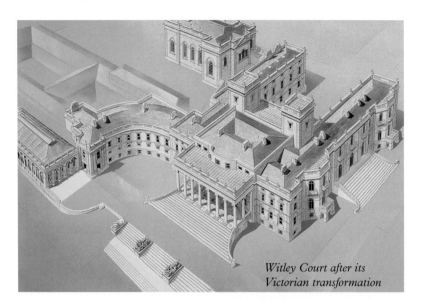

*Witley Court after its Victorian transformation*

The simple, even austere, neo-classical idiom which Nash had used on the exterior was already out of fashion, and so Ward now commissioned the architect Samuel Whitfield Daukes (1811–80) to remodel the house in the more ornate Italianate style used in 1845–8 for the creation of Osborne House on the Isle of Wight for Queen Victoria. Daukes was not a particularly well-known architect (he had trained in York before starting a practice in Gloucester in 1837, where he became the architect of the railway linking the city with Birmingham), but he had proved his familiarity with the Italianate style in his rebuilding of Abberley Hall near Witley in 1845–6. No doubt it was this local connection which drew him to Lord Ward's attention, although by the time he was

## SERVICES AND TECHNOLOGY

*I*n its heyday, Witley Court was a classic example of how a Victorian country house functioned. 'Below stairs', the basement (really the ground floor) extended under the entire house except for the west wing. It was a labyrinth of mostly small rooms, with the main service passage running from the large square kitchen, immediately behind the grand staircase, to the Butler's Pantry beneath the main Dining Room on the east front. Midway between the two was the Housekeeper's Room, occupying the space under the Saloon, while adjoining it under the south portico was a Still Room for storing and possibly making jams and other preserves (this is still there). Also on this level were the Butler's Room and Maids' Sitting Room. Beneath the Ballroom was a long tiled room, probably used as a dairy, and below everything was a subterranean floor.

A very extensive area to the west of the main house was also given over to services of various kinds. The servants' hall stood behind the curving south-west wing, with the Dudley children's schoolroom above. To the north of the Kitchen Court was a three-storey wing; this contained more service rooms on the ground floor, servants' bedrooms on the first floor, and a second-floor-level corridor connecting the house to the church. Extending west from the Kitchen Court were three further service courtyards, ending in the stables. Beyond the stable yard stood a gigantic coal stack, maintained at around 1,500 tons (tonnes), which fed five hot-water boilers and the dozens of fireplaces in the house. A track in a tunnel connected the coal stack to a cellar beneath the house. One of the boilers worked a hot-air central-heating system, much in advance of its time, which warmed the house and church. The house could consume as much as 30 tons of coal per day – Dudley coal, of course, brought from the Black Country by barge to Shrawley on the River Severn and carried the remaining four miles by the horses and carts of tenant farmers.

*The laundry staff of Witley Court in the Service Courtyard*

commissioned he had already moved his practice to London. His only other country house was Horsted Place, Sussex (1850-2), in Tudor style, although he was also responsible for the Royal Agricultural College at Cirencester, likewise Tudor, and the buildings which form the nucleus of the present University of Gloucestershire in Cheltenham, in austere Gothic.

The transformation of Witley involved the recasting of the entire exterior (including the adjoining church) in Bath stone to match Nash's porticos, which were the only existing features left untouched. Yet again the house was re-roofed, this time with a flat-pitched lead roof concealed by a balustraded parapet. A new curving wing was added at the south-west corner, leading to an enormous glass-roofed conservatory which replaced the more modest one added by Nash. The elaborate gardens designed by W A Nesfield are described below. Inside the house the Georgian interiors gave way to a fashionable cosmetic modernisation, grafted onto existing walls and designed by Moxons, the royal decorators. Extensive use was made of mouldings in Carton Pierre, a kind of strengthened papier mache. Although the entrance hall was relatively restrained, the main reception rooms, including the vast Ballroom, were in variations of the white-and-gold 'Tous les Louis' decoration (inspired by French interiors of the reigns of Louis XIV and XV)

much favoured by the English nouveaux riches. Many of the marble chimneypieces and other embellishments were carved by James Forsyth, author of the Perseus and Andromeda fountain. In the east wing Daukes installed a so-called fire-proof floor of steel girders and concrete – probably intended as much as anything to support the additional weight created by the stone-cladding – which was to prove completely ineffective in the 1937 fire. The upper floor of the west wing, originally the Long Gallery, was remodelled to create a top-lit Picture Gallery (though it is possible this had already happened under Nash, who created such galleries at Buckingham Palace and Attingham Hall in

*The top-lit Picture Gallery with its characteristic Victorian clutter*

*William Humble Ward, first Earl of Dudley, of the second creation, for whom Witley and its gardens were completely remodelled*

*A postcard of the Perseus and Andromeda fountain in operation, postmarked 1910*

*Georgina, Countess of Dudley, wife of the first earl, known for her beauty*

Shropshire). In addition to some fine French, Italian and Flemish pieces, old photographs show much standard mid-Victorian upholstered seating as well as reproduction Boulle items that would have chimed with the Frenchified decoration.

In 1860, the year that the transformation was completed, the earldom of Dudley was revived and conferred on Lord Ward in recognition of his generosity to local charities (as well, no doubt, as his immense wealth). In 1865 he married Georgina Elizabeth Moncrieffe, a lady of 'peerless' beauty, by whom he had six sons and one daughter. The earl died in 1885 at the age of 67, but his widow survived until 1929, famous locally for her stately bearing, good looks and charm. Their son the second earl (also named William) inherited aged eighteen

and did not take up residence at Witley until he was 21, when there were lavish festivities lasting three days. These were repeated in 1891 when he married Rachel Anne Gurney, a Norfolk banking heiress who was later described as having 'the beauty of an Eastern Queen'.

*Rachel, Countess of Dudley, dressed as Queen Esther for a ball held in 1897 to celebrate Queen Victoria's Diamond Jubilee*

## THE SECOND EARL'S 21ST BIRTHDAY CELEBRATIONS

The celebrations for the young second earl's coming-of-age in 1888 were spread over three days. On 7th August he and his mother received successive congratulatory deputations from the tenants of the Witley Court and Holt estates, and in the evening there was a splendid ball for 'the county', attended by 214 guests. For this, a 60-foot (18-metre) marquee was erected in the grounds. Both drives were illuminated by hurricane lamps, and fairy lights bordered the lawns. Another marquee accommodated the guests' coachmen, while a huge temporary stable was provided for 100 horses.

The next day there were further congratulations from deputations of tradesmen (both local and from London), presented in the Picture Gallery. The third day was given over to entertaining the tenantry on a grand scale. The drives were decorated with flags and bunting and an even larger marquee, over 200 feet (60 metres) long, was erected in the park, in which nearly 900 male

cottagers sat down to an ample lunch washed down with plentiful supplies of beer. There was also a full-scale fair, complete with merry-go-rounds, swing-boats, Punch-and-Judy shows and demonstrations of juggling and ventriloquism. Pleasure boats floated on the Front Pool and the fountains played for an hour in the afternoon.

*The second earl in 1888, with his mother and siblings; he is thought to be wearing the uniform of the Worcestershire Regiment*

*The second earl aged eighteen, when still Viscount Ednam*

Tea was served to 416 children and 427 mothers and other village women, followed by dancing to the accompaniment of two bands. As dusk fell the fountains were illuminated and the evening came to a climax with an elaborate firework display.

At the height of the family's prosperity the Dudleys owned properties and estates in London (Dudley House and 7 Carlton Gardens), Cheshire, Scotland, Wales, Ireland, Boulogne, Nice, Rome, Vienna and Jamaica. By 1883 the estates totalled 25,554 acres (10,300 hectares), of which over 14,000 acres (5,700 hectares) were in Worcestershire. Life at Witley was correspondingly opulent, and reached a zenith during the 1890s, when the second earl's friend the Prince of Wales (later King Edward VII) became a regular visitor. He and his entourage were attracted particularly by Lord Dudley's elaborate shooting parties. The park had a staff of 25 full-time gamekeepers who maintained a stock of partridges, pheasants and deer for these occasions. Mrs Berkeley, who as a young woman was often invited to the Court, later recalled, 'One side of the gay life I loathed, the game question. The battues, the wholesale slaughter of tame birds driven into a corner, the crowd of keepers, the destroyed crops, the ravaged pasture land, and what all these things meant to the farmers on the estate'. In 1895, a golf course was laid out for the further entertainment of guests.

During the grand house parties the house would be full to bursting with family, staff and guests. The latter would stay for up to a week, bringing with them their own servants, who also had to be accommodated – a valet for each

gentleman and a personal maid for each lady – to organise their frequent changes of clothing during the day. Some guests even brought their own cook. The Prince of Wales, often travelling without his wife Princess Alexandra, had a large retinue which might include his personal loaders for the shooting. A day of sporting activities created substantial appetites, which were gratified by enormous dinners, held, when numbers required, in the Ballroom or Picture Gallery.

*A bedroom panelled in French-polished satinwood, photographed in 1920*

*A royal shooting party at Witley: in the centre the Prince of Wales (later Edward VII), and, standing to the left of him, the second Earl of Dudley (in white waistcoat) and his first wife, Rachel*

*One of the young twin sons of the second earl, astride a sculpture of a lion on the South Portico steps*

G STANSFIELD COLLECTION

This way of life was supported by a permanent staff of some 50 servants, presided over by the butler. He was in charge of the indoor male staff and responsible for the service of meals, drinks and the smooth running of the household generally. The housekeeper took her orders from the countess and, via an army of housemaids, dealt with all cleaning duties. Of equal rank were the head cook and head gardener, each of whom had a large staff that brought the total complement to over 100.

## THE END OF AN ERA

*Gertie Millar (far right), who later became Lady Dudley, on a postcard with other popular showgirls in 1906*

As befitted his wealth and connections, the second earl was appointed to a succession of public offices, including Lord Lieutenant of Ireland (1902–5), Privy Councillor and, finally, Governor General of Australia (1908–11). Although he and his wife had seven children, born between 1892 and 1907, they were very

MARY EVANS PICTURE LIBRARY

different people, with different attitudes to life. While Lord Dudley was gregarious and very much part of the Prince of Wales's racy circle, Lady Dudley preferred the solid Victorian values of duty, home, family and church, and was much given to good works. Eventually cracks began to appear in the marriage and in 1908 a legal separation was agreed, with Witley Court settled on the countess. She took a great interest in the gardens, laying out an area with clipped topiary known as 'My Lady's Garden' which is now the garden of the Church tearooms. On Sunday mornings she would lead her staff in a stately procession through the house to church.

Meanwhile, as a result of foreign competition, the Dudley wealth was on the wane. Between 1889 and 1913 the earl is known to have mortgaged the estate and sold pictures to fund his extravagant entertaining. When Lady Dudley was tragically drowned in a swimming accident at the family house in County Galway in 1920, he immediately decided to sell the Witley estate. In 1924 he married his second wife, a former Gaiety Girl named Gertie Millar, moved back to Himley Hall and died in 1932. The Dudley family line continues, even though its connection with Witley has long ceased.

## THE FINAL YEARS

The new owner in 1920 was another rich industrialist aspiring to the status of landed gentry, Sir Herbert Smith. Born in Kidderminster in 1872, Smith worked his way up through the ailing carpet manufacturer Humphries, becoming general manager in 1906 and, after turning the company's finances around, buying it in 1910. In 1920 he set up a conglomerate, Carpet Trades Ltd, receiving a baronetcy in the same year (for services as chairman of the Carpet Rationing Committee in the First World War) and retiring a millionaire two years later, aged 49. Although his corpulent physique earned him the unflattering nickname 'Piggy', he came from a musical family and was an accomplished violinist. He acquired Witley Court furnished but, although he expended money in installing electricity, he also reduced staff levels (to just half-a-dozen maids and a butler) and retreated to the south-west corner, effectively abandoning parts of the house. Its existence as a rich man's home was brought to an abrupt end by the devastating fire which broke out at about 8pm on 7 September 1937, while Sir Herbert was away. Starting, it would seem, in the servants' quarters on the top floor and fanned by a strong wind, the fire spread rapidly to the main rooms of the mansion. Little could be done to quell the flames since the hydrant system connected to the fountain reservoir had not been maintained and Daukes's 'fire-proof' floors proved useless. Only a handful of staff were in the building, and, although with the help of villagers many of the contents were saved, the central and eastern sections were gutted. It was, wrote a reporter from a local paper, 'a fine but awful spectacle'. When it turned out that insurance money would pay for no more than a quarter of the cost of rebuilding, Smith decided to dispose of the property. No one was ever to live in the house again. The surviving contents and many garden ornaments were auctioned over eight days in the autumn of 1938, followed by the sale of the house itself the following year to a Mr Banks for a mere £4,000. The land was sold off separately for agriculture, and standing timber was felled.

THE FIRE IN PROGRESS AT WITLEY COURT

An aerial view of Witley Court taken yesterday shows the extent of the conflagration. The front portion of of the picture were virtually burnt out. The flames did not reach the chapel shown in

### RUIN AND RESURRECTION

The Court changed hands again in 1954, being bought by an antique dealer from Stratford-upon-Avon who stripped and sold anything of value that remained – marble chimneypieces from the ravaged interior, lead, slates and timber from the roof, statuary from the garden and heavy plate-glass from the conservatory. Ruin rapidly overtook the structure, with trees growing up through the floors, and in the 1950s and 1960s it narrowly survived demolition and associated proposals for a motor-racing circuit,

caravan park and housing estate. The church might have been bodily removed to London, while the Perseus and Andromeda fountain nearly ended up on a traffic island outside Worcester Cathedral. However, the issuing of a Building Preservation Order provided vital protection in 1964, followed in 1970 by scheduling of the house and surroundings as an Ancient Monument. Once the Department of the Environment had served a compulsory guardianship order in 1972, work to arrest further decay could begin – a challenge continued since 1984 by English Heritage.

*Sir Herbert ('Piggy') Smith, self-made millionaire and owner of Witley Court at the time of the fire*

*Left: The fire takes hold and, above, as reported in the local press*

*Witley Court in 1969, trees growing within its walls*

# THE GARDENS OF WITLEY COURT

*Andromeda, from the South Parterre fountain*

*Opposite: A view in the woodland walks, looking towards the cascade*

*Witley Court in the 1770s as portrayed by E Dayes. Note the causeway carrying the drive across Front Pool and the service blocks to right and left of the entrance*

Very little is known of the early gardens of Witley Court, although it can certainly be assumed that they were formal. Almost the only piece of evidence is the late seventeenth-century painting illustrated on page 18, which shows walled compartments on the slope below the south front. The 1732 estate map shows the area to the south of this subdivided into fields, with the extensive deer park (perhaps that referred to in the sixteenth century) lying to the west, but by 1772 Isaac Taylor's map of Worcestershire shows the parkland extending to the south as well. The first Lord Foley also acquired land to the north so that an appropriately grand approach could be created on that side, with an axial causeway and bridge across Front Pool, newly formed by damming the Shrawley Brook. A formal avenue was laid out to the east, crossing a ravine by another causeway.

Between 1772 and 1793/4 an ornamental woodland known as the Wilderness was developed north-east of the house, with walks laid out along the banks of Front Pool and Shrawley Brook. Ornamental plantations were also laid out to enhance the park, although

under 'Lord Balloon' (Thomas Foley VI) poor management seems to have resulted in problems with waterlogging and consequent growth of rushes. This was addressed by his successor (Thomas VII), who called in John Nash to remodel the house, and the leading landscape designer Humphry Repton to redesign its setting. On the south and east fronts the house was surrounded by a new raised terrace and simple flower beds, while on the north side the formal causeway was removed in favour of curving carriage drives leading out to the turnpike road. The park was extended east to include Warford Pool and, more generally, the condition of the land was improved by means of better drainage and the introduction of a herd of bullocks to eat the rushes.

The most dramatic transformation of the setting of Witley Court came in 1854–60, when the first Earl of Dudley commissioned W A Nesfield to design new gardens that would complement the Italianate revamping of the mansion being carried out under Samuel Daukes. Nesfield was probably introduced to Dudley by Lady Emily Foley, for whom he was designing gardens at Stoke Edith near Hereford. By October 1854, when he came to Witley for three days to confer about the project, Nesfield had established himself as the leading garden designer of his generation and was advising some of the wealthiest landowners in the country; however, he was later to refer to the gardens at Witley as his 'monster work'. Like those by Nash and Repton which they replaced, they were intended to provide a suitable setting for the south and east fronts of the mansion and were in a correspondingly Italianate manner.

On the south front a flight of steps with curved balustrade connected Nash's portico with the grandiose parterre, which was separated

WORCESER RECORD OFFICE

*The South Parterre
in 1880*

*Nesfield's watercolour
of the South Parterre, with
the fountains playing*

from the deer park beyond by a ha-ha (or concealed ditch) and stone balustrade. From the terrace a broad central gravel walk led down the slope to the quatrefoil-shaped pool at the centre of the parterre, in the middle of which rose the monumental fountain depicting the mythological tale of Perseus and Andromeda. This was designed by Nesfield (a sheet of modifications to the design is dated 1858) and installed in 1860. In line with his belief that the immediate setting of a house should be as formal as possible, the gravel walk was flanked by symmetrical beds of flowers and shrubs outlined with raised stone kerbs (Nesfield preferred these to the usual clipped box if the budget allowed), all embedded in smooth turf. Vertical emphasis was provided by a formal dotting of clipped standard trees. The fountain pool was surrounded by its own symmetrical setting of flower and shrub beds, further diversified by standard trees and large flower-filled stone vases or 'tazzas'. A cross-walk terminated by ornate stone pavilions (also designed by Nesfield) separated this area from the large semicircular lawn that rose up the far slope, which had its own stone-edged parterres and specimen trees and shrubs. Crowning the rise, and terminating the main axis through the garden, were the

G STANSFIELD COLLECTION/NESFIELD ARCHIVE

ornate 'Golden Gates' – not part of Nesfield's original design, but introduced in 1862 in a position where he had intended a belvedere or viewing platform.

Below the east front was a smaller garden containing a more conventional parterre. This featured all the elements of a 'parterre de broderie', a design of seventeenth-century French origin which emulates the patterns of embroidery – plant-like motifs of scrolls, volutes and rays, laid out with box and filled in with flowers and coloured gravels. Nesfield's palette for the latter included red (achieved with crushed brick and tile), white (Derbyshire spar) and blue (Westmorland slate). Once again, there were clipped evergreens, ornamental shrubs and tazzas filled with flowers, and a large fountain – the fountain of Flora, goddess of Spring – as the centrepiece. At a lower level, between the east and south parterres, was a long flower border designed as a guilloche or ribbon.

The scale of the Witley gardens, and particularly the fountains, attracted attention from the start, with a succession of gardening correspondents publishing their impressions in various journals. Changing tastes meant that Nesfield's style began to go out of favour in the 1870s. The *Gardeners' Chronicle* in 1872 considered that 'its very magnitude is imposing, but the style of decoration is frittered and childish. It is barbarous in its magnificence, highly irritating and unsatisfactory'. The *Cottage Gardener* in the same year was kinder, conceding that 'embroidered gardens have of late become less fashionable', but concluding

*The lion sculptures which once embellished the steps of the South Portico*

# WILLIAM ANDREWS NESFIELD (1794–1881)

*Portrait of Nesfield by John Duffield Harding, c. 1840*

The son of a Church of England vicar, Nesfield was intended to follow his father and grandfather into the Church. A meeting with a cousin who was an army officer led to a change of heart, however, and after two terms at Trinity College, Cambridge, he studied architectural perspective, engineering and map-making at the Royal Military Academy at Woolwich. He served in the Peninsula Campaigns in Spain and then in the Niagara Region in Canada. On his return to England he resigned his army commission to become a professional watercolour painter.

It was on the advice of his brother-in-law, the architect Anthony Salvin, that he had a further change of direction and turned to landscape gardening. He began by designing formal gardens to accompany the Elizabethan and Jacobean-style houses which Salvin was working on at the time, but he soon became sufficiently sussessful to practise independently. He strove to transfer the art of painting into his garden designs, using what he described as 'Nature's Materials' – not only trees, shrubs and flowers, but also rocks and minerals – to add colour to his parterres during the winter months. His designs were intricate and elegant, with a subtle blending of colours very different from the garish planting generally associated with large Victorian formal gardens. Using grand French layouts of the late sixteenth and early seventeenth centuries as his inspiration, he believed that the immediate environs of a house should be as formal as possible, with boundaries marked by balustrades and gates. Beyond them he liked to open up the landscape to reveal distant prospects of hills, not hesitating to adopt what he called 'the judicial use of the axe' where he considered it necessary.

*A triton, part of the Flora fountain*

*The South Parterre as recreated in spring 2003*

*'My Lady's Garden', laid out for Rachel, the wife of the second earl. The topiary has since disappeared*

that 'here fancy work of this description is so well blended with masses of rhododendrons and other shrubs, which in their turn are enlivened with sculptural objects judiciously placed, that the whole can hardly fail to please the most fastidious'. There is evidence that in the 1880s the internal form and colour of Nesfield's layout began to change as successive head gardeners moved away from the original relatively sophisticated planting, towards the more exuberant bedding-out beloved of later

Victorians – one large bed, for instance, contained 5,000 geraniums set off by yellow calceolarias and blue lobelia. It was at this point that the parterres on the south slope were replanted with shrubs to provide a frame for the vista to the Golden Gates. In this period, too, a smaller garden of clipped topiary was laid out (in the former kitchen garden orchard) to the west of the house for the wife of the second Earl of Dudley, Rachel, and named after her. Meanwhile, the clipped standards in the main parterres continued to grow imperceptibly larger, until they tended to dominate the overall picture when the fountains were not playing. Numerous old photographs and postcards document the gradually evolving face of the gardens in these decades.

After 1900 Lord Dudley's deteriorating financial situation (reflecting his lavish spending as well as the declining iron industry) meant that less money was available to keep up the gardens, a situation exacerbated by the First World War. The planting of the flower beds was simplified, and photographs taken in 1920 show that, although the lawns continued to be

NATIONAL MONUMENTS RECORD

G STANSFIELD COLLECTION

G STANSFIELD COLLECTION

*The punt house on the north side of Front Pool*

*Above left: Family visitors by Front Pool in the early 1900s*

*Left: Dicks (Lady Morveth), Patsie (Lady Alexandra Patricia), and 'self' (Lady Gladys Honour), the three daughters of the second earl on the frozen Front Pool*

mown, the edges of the beds were not trimmed as they had been. In this state of reduced maintenance the gardens continued until the disastrous fire of 1937, after which upkeep ceased and the stripping of saleable features began – the Golden Gates, for instance, were sold to Arizona, while offers for the fountains were received at one time or another from Bing Crosby and Billy Butlin.

The eighteenth-century Wilderness and the pools on the north side of the house seem to have been untouched by Nesfield, but in the 1870s and 1880s the valley seems to have been extensively planted with American plants and ornamental trees, along with a profusion of spring-flowering bulbs and plants. Below the dam a footbridge took the ornamental walk across the Shrawley Brook, reinstated in timber and stone in 1999. A rustic timber boathouse was built on the southern side of the small western arm of Front Pool, probably before 1914, and this was repaired by English Heritage in 1999. On the north side of the Pool a stone and brick underground boathouse is set into a steep field-slope. This was used as a punt-house, although its construction date is uncertain. A major sale of standing timber in 1938 resulted in the felling of the majority of the woodland enclosing the park, and few areas were replanted. After the sale of the land between Front Pool and the public road – North Park or Pool House estate – its new private owner planted a screen of conifers which

effectively blocked the view of Witley Court from the north. Since its acquisition by English Heritage in 1996 (with help from the Heritage Lottery Fund), the view has been opened up again and new visitor facilities have been developed in the area. This is also where a new Wilderness Garden has been created.

*The recently repaired rustic boathouse*

## FURTHER READING

Mavis Batey and David Lambert: *The English Garden Tour* (1990)

Shirley Evans: *Nesfield's Monster Work: The gardens of Witley Court* (1994)

Terry Friedman: *James Gibbs* (1984)

Mark Girouard: *Life in the English Country House* (1978)

Mark Girouard: *The Victorian Country House* (1979)

John Harris: 'Ichnographica Domestica' (*Architectural History* XIV, 1971)

Christopher Hussey: 'Witley Court' (*Country Life*, 15 June 1945)

Alistair Laing: 'Foreign Decorators and Plasterers in England' (in *The Rococo in England*, ed. C Hind, 1986)

Bill Pardoe: *Witley Court & Church* (1986)

John Summerson: *The Life and Works of John Nash* (1980)

M J Tooley: *William Andrews Nesfield, A Bicentenary Exhibition Guide* (1994)

R O Walker: *Witley, Worcestershire* (1990)

*Guide to Witley Parish Church*, Witley Parish Church Committee (1999)

*Visit our website at*
**www.english-heritage.org.uk**

*Published by English Heritage, 1 Waterhouse Square, 138–142 Holborn, London EC1N 2ST*
*Copyright © English Heritage 2003.*
*First published by English Heritage 2003, reprinted 2006*

*Unless otherwise stated photographs are copyright English Heritage, and were taken by Mike Hesketh-Roberts, Peter Williams, James Davies and Damian Grady (aerial photograph) of the English Heritage photographic unit.*

*Edited by Susannah Charlton*
*Designed by Joanna Griffiths*
*Picture Researcher: Diana Phillips*
*Production Manager: Richard Jones*
*Printed by the colourhouse*
*C60, 7/06, Product code 03783, ISBN 1-85074 845 4*

Acknowledgements
*This guide draws considerably on the previous guidebook written by Richard Gray, with contributions by Shirley Evans (on Nesfield's garden) and Jeremy Musson. This has been augmented by Stanley Jenkins's researches, and by recent research carried out for English Heritage by Dr Pat Hughes and Ron Shoesmith, with the valuable input of Dr Glyn Coppack, and Tony Fleming. The picture researcher would like to thank Graham Stansfield, Dr Johnson, Mrs Watkins and Ruth Butler for help with their picture collections.*